EMPIRE *containing y*e *Artick lands near Hudsons*

BAFFINS
BAY

ARCTIC

NEW NORTH
WALES

NEW SOUTH
WALES

HUDSONS
BAY

TERRA
LABRADOR

NEW
BRITAIN

NEW
FOUND
LAND

The Main
Bank

False
Bank

act of Land
of Wild Bulls

LAKE SUPERIOR

LAKE HURONS

LAKE
ILINOIS

LAKE
ERIE

NEW FRANCE

PENN

VIRGINIA

CAROLINA

OF THE ENGLISH EMPIRE

CapeCod

Bermudas or
Summer Islands

THE GOLF

BAY

MEXICO

INDIAN

SEA

CARIBY
ISLANDS

UNDER ★ MY ★ WINGS ★

· VOICES · *from* COLONIAL AMERICA

EVERY ★ THING ★ ★ PROSPERS ★

LOUISIANA

1682—1803

RICHARD WORTH

WITH

KEVIN D. ROBERTS, PH.D., CONSULTANT

NATIONAL GEOGRAPHIC

WASHINGTON, D.C.

John M. Fahey, Jr., *President and Chief Executive Officer*
Gilbert M. Grosvenor, *Chairman of the Board*
Nina D. Hoffman, *Executive Vice President,*
 President of Books and Education Publishing Group
Ericka Markman, *Senior Vice President, President of*
 Children's Books and Education Publishing Group
Stephen Mico, *Senior Vice President and Publisher,*
 Children's Books and Education Publishing Group

STAFF FOR THIS BOOK
Nancy Laties Feresten, *Vice President, Editor-in-Chief*
 of Children's Books
Suzanne Patrick Fonda, *Project Editor*
Robert D. Johnston, Ph.D., *Associate Professor and Director,*
 Teaching of History Program University of Illinois at Chicago,
 Series Editor
Bea Jackson, *Design Director, Children's Books and Education*
 Publishing Group
Jim Hiscott, *Art Director*
Jean Cantu, *Illustrations Specialist*
Carl Mehler, *Director of Maps*
Justin Morrill and Martin S. Walz, *Map Research,*
 Design, and Production
Margery Towery, *Indexer*
Rebecca Hinds, *Managing Editor*
R. Gary Colbert, *Production Director*
Lewis R. Bassford, *Production Manager*
Vincent P. Ryan and Maryclare Tracy, *Manufacturing Managers*

Voices from Colonial Louisiana was prepared by
CREATIVE MEDIA APPLICATIONS, INC.
Richard Worth, *Writer*
Fabia Wargin Design, Inc., *Design and Production*
Matt Levine, *Editor*
Susan Madoff, *Associate Editor*
Laurie Lieb, *Copyeditor*
Jennifer Bright, *Image Researcher*

Body text is set in Deepdene, sidebars are Caslon 337 Oldstyle, and display text is Cochin Archaic Bold.

LIBRARY OF CONGRESS CATALOGING-IN-PUBLICATION DATA
Worth, Richard.
 Voices from colonial America. Louisiana, 1682–1803 / by Richard Worth.
  p. cm. — (Voices from colonial America)
 Includes bibliographical references and index.
 ISBN 0-7922-6544-0 (Hardcover)
 ISBN 0-7922-6850-4 (Library)
1. Louisiana—History—To 1803—Juvenile literature. I. Title. II. Series.
 F372.W67 2005
 976.3'01—dc22

                                    2005016225

Printed in Belgium

CONTENTS

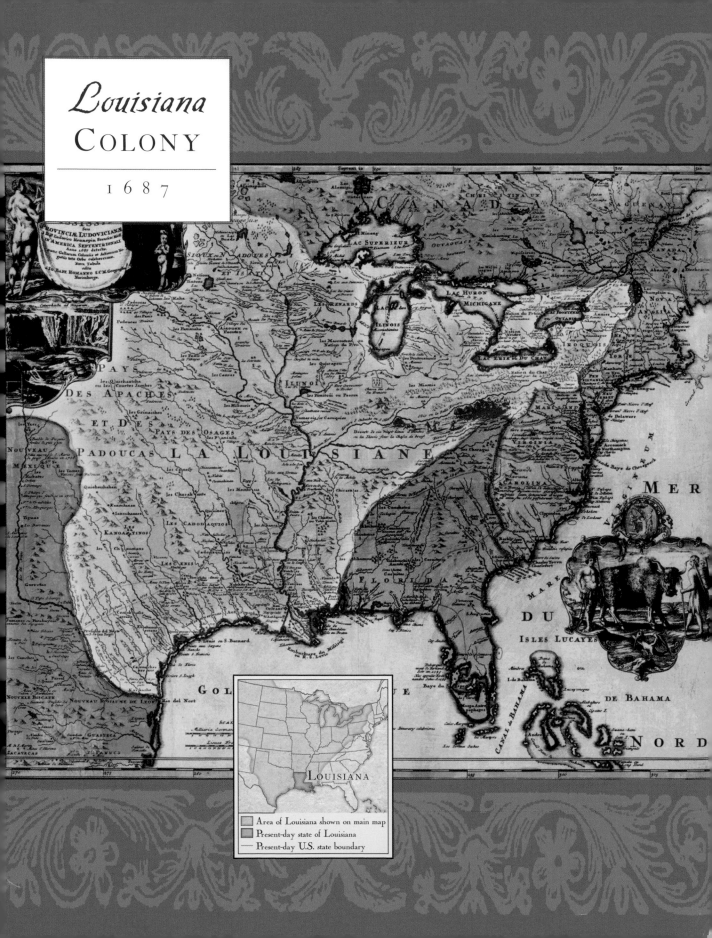

Louisiana
COLONY
1687

Area of Louisiana shown on main map

Present-day state of Louisiana

Present-day U.S. state boundary

LOUISIANA

INTRODUCTION

by

Kevin D. Roberts, Ph.D.

A 19th-century watercolor of a lush plantation in Louisiana
by artist Adrian Persac

Our modern sensibilities make it very difficult to imagine
what Louisiana looked, sounded, smelled, and felt like four
hundred years ago. Today, interstates crisscross the swamps,
major cities populate the rolling hills, and bustling commerce dominates the coast. Neither the native peoples nor

OPPOSITE: The area drained by the Mississippi River that made up
France's Lousiana Province has been highlighted in yellow on this 1687 map
by Father Louis Hennepin. The present-day state of Louisiana appears in the
inset for comparison.

the European settlers who lived then could have imagined the landscape of the present-day state of Louisiana.

For historians, the most difficult part of our job is bringing the past to life. To recreate colonial Louisiana is to trace its evolution as a place once dominated by significant native cultures, to its emergence as an outpost in the Atlantic world, to its ultimate prominence as a strategic and economic center in the Americas. Perhaps the one constant throughout all of that change has been Louisiana's cultural diversity and social uniqueness. Different Indian, European, and African peoples converged—and sometimes collided, violently—in ways that created a distinctive society. Even the interstates, cities, and cell phone towers that now dot Louisiana have not changed that fundamental aspect of Louisiana's unique society and history.

Therefore, the period when that cultural hodgepodge was created is essential to our understanding of both Louisiana history and modern Louisiana society. From the struggles endured by the early French settlers to the seemingly impossible task of the Spanish to assimilate Louisiana into their empire in 1763, the story of colonial Louisiana is filled with failure and tragedy. Ironically, not until the arrival of thousands of African slaves—whose own story, of course, was pure tragedy—did the colony of Louisiana stabilize economically. Indeed, without the rise of sugar and cotton production in the early 1790s, it is difficult to see colonial Louisiana becoming more than a blip on the map of colonial America. But that newfound success, as well as the colony's strategic location, made the Louisiana Purchase in 1803 the exclamation point on colonial Louisiana's history.

As a native Louisianan, I am particularly delighted to serve as the historical consultant for *Voices from Colonial America: Louisiana*. In fact, my own passion for history began at a middle school in humid southern Louisiana, where I tried to imagine the difficulties my Acadian ancestors experienced on their way to the colony. This book will take you back in time and vividly recreate life in early Louisiana for you. I know that you will find it to be a fascinating place. Enjoy your trip.

The French flag is raised in the port of New Orleans for the last time in 1803, just before the transfer of ownership of Louisiana to the United States, in this 19th-century painting called "Raising the Colours for the Last Time, the Cessation of New Orleans in 1803."

CHAPTER ONE

La Salle Founds Louisiana

SIEUR DE LA SALLE LEADS AN EXPEDITION *of French explorers along the Mississippi River and establishes a new colony called Louisiana.*

uring the 17th century, French explorers carved out a large empire in North America. They called the land New France. Although the name New France originally referred to all French claims on the continent of North America, it was also used for the region around the St. Lawrence River and the Great Lakes

OPPOSITE: In this painting, Sieur de La Salle claims possession of Louisiana and the Mississippi in the name of King Louis XIV of France in 1682. He has marked the location of his announcement with a pillar upon which the French coat of arms appears.

in what is now Canada. Here, the French traded with Native American tribes for furs—primarily beaver fur— along the Great Lakes. Beaver fur was very valuable in Europe, especially for making warm hats and decorating the clothing of the very rich.

The French wanted to increase their fur-trading empire south along the Mississippi River. By 1682 France claimed all of the land drained by the Mississippi River— an area that extended from the Great Lakes to the Gulf of Mexico and from the Rocky Mountains to the Appalachians. They named this vast area Louisiana. The north-central part of it (the area that includes the present-day states of Illinois, Indiana, and part of Missouri) was called Illinois Country. The region around the Ohio River—Ohio Country—was also claimed by England. The area along the Mississippi River south of Illinois Country and along the Gulf Coast became the most heavily settled. It is this area—the present-day states of Louisiana and Mississippi and part of Alabama—that formed the core of France's Louisiana territory. The French plan was to build a string of forts to connect the various parts of its empire in the New World (as Europeans called the Americas). The forts would protect French fur traders and settlements, prevent English colonists along the Atlantic seaboard from moving westward, and strengthen France's foothold in North America.

La Salle Explores the Mississippi River

The story of Louisiana begins with René-Robert Cavelier, Sieur de La Salle. In February 1682, La Salle led an expedition of about 50 French explorers south from New France. The explorers were forced to carry their canoes southward from the shores of Lake Michigan because the rivers of the north were still frozen with thick ice. Eventually, the explorers reached a point where there was open water. They launched their canoes and paddled down the Illinois River, which emptied into the broad Mississippi.

Sieur—an archaic French title, comparable to "sir"

In 1682, La Salle's ship sails into the rough waters of the mouth of the Mississippi River.

The Life of LA SALLE

BORN IN ROUEN, FRANCE, IN 1643, RENÉ-ROBERT CAVELIER de La Salle grew up in a well-to-do family. He attended a Jesuit (a Catholic religious order) college. However, his Jesuit instructors soon realized that he was not cut out to become a priest. They called him *"stubborn, domineering and hot tempered."* Soon afterward, La Salle left the Jesuit order and decided to travel to New France.

La Salle arrived in New France in 1666. He received a large plot of land outside the French town of Montréal. Soon, he began planting crops and trading with the local Native Americans. The French carried on a brisk trade with the Indians in beaver pelts and moose hides. Although La Salle made money on the fur trade, he was far more interested in the possibilities of exploring the interior of North America.

The French explorers paddled large canoes, about 24 feet (7.3 m) long. These boats could carry roughly 1,500 pounds (680 kg) —food, trade goods for the Indians who lived along the river, and several men to work the paddles. The strong ribs of the canoes were built of boards made from ash and cedar trees. The ribs were covered in bark stripped from birch trees. These sturdy canoes could cover as much as 100 miles (160 km) per day.

French explorers had already sailed along Lake Huron and Lake Superior, which were located west of the

St. Lawrence River and considered part of New France. In fact, from 1669 to 1671, La Salle had led his own expedition along the Great Lakes and the Ohio River. Two years later, French explorers Jacques Marquette and Louis Joliet had paddled from Lake Michigan down the Mississippi River. Joliet believed that the Mississippi River flowed southward and emptied into the Gulf of Mexico. Spanish ships had already traveled this coastal area. France wanted to claim the Gulf of Mexico and the Mississippi River before the Spanish established settlements there. From the Gulf, French ships could carry furs from the Mississippi River back to France.

DOWN THE MISSISSIPPI

After studying Joliet's maps, La Salle decided to return to Europe and obtain permission from King Louis XIV to launch an expedition to follow along the Mississippi River to its mouth.

La Salle returned to New France in 1678 to begin preparations for his expedition. He was accompanied by his friend Henry de Tonti. In March 1681, La Salle and Tonti visited the Native American tribes along the southern shores of the Great Lakes. La Salle journeyed to the Indian villages, where he convinced the chiefs to sign peace treaties. La Salle hoped that peaceful Indian tribes would protect the area along the Great Lakes in the name of France.

Henry de Tonti

Henry de Tonti was born in France to a successful Italian family in 1650. In 1668, he joined the French Army and later commanded troops on board naval warships. During a bloody battle in Sicily, Tonti lost part of his hand when he was struck by a bomb. He cut off the rest of his hand with his own knife. Afterward, he was fitted with an iron hand that he always kept covered with a glove. Consequently, the Native Americans called Tonti "Iron Hand."

Tonti accompanied La Salle in his voyage down the Mississippi River in 1682. Soon afterward, Tonti built Fort St. Louis on the Illinois River in Illinois Country. He served as the commander of the fort until 1700. On a visit to Louisiana in 1704, Tonti died of yellow fever.

In 1682, La Salle, assisted by Tonti, led an expedition southward along the Mississippi River. The explorers passed the place where the waters of the Missouri River emptied into the Mississippi. They continued their journey to a point near the present-day city of Memphis, Tennessee. La Salle decided to build a fort there and left some of his men to defend it. La Salle's foresight placed Fort Prud'homme at a strategic point in the region where it would serve to defend France's claims to the Mississippi River. The expedition continued southward. Along the way, La Salle encountered Indian tribes, including the Yazoo, the Arkansas, and the Choctaw.

FOUNDING LOUISIANA

By April 6, 1682, La Salle and his men had reached the mouth of the Mississippi River. Here, the river channels cut through the mud, forming a delta. One group, headed by Tonti, paddled along one of the large channels of the delta while La Salle explored another channel. On April 9, after the two groups met up again, La Salle put up a large stone pillar. On it were the words *"Louis the Great, King of France . . . reigns the 9th of April, 1682."* Claiming all the land along the Mississippi and along any waterways flowing into it, La Salle named it Louisiana, after the French king.

By the time La Salle erected the stone pillar, the expedition was running short of food. La Salle soon became sick with a terrible fever. Nevertheless, with Tonti's help, the expedition headed northward to establish more forts on the Mississippi River to protect the area from Indians. La Salle eventually recovered his health and continued his explorations of the Mississippi River until his death in 1687.

THE NATIVE AMERICANS OF LOUISIANA

La Salle's claim to the land he called Louisiana also included possession of all the native peoples who lived there. The Native American tribes that La Salle encountered during his expeditions had already been living in the area for hundreds of years. Among the tribes were the Yazoo and their close relatives, the Tunica. The Yazoo hunted and fished along the Mississippi River. They lived in small villages, where they were organized into groups called clans.

Another tribe that La Salle encountered was the Natchez. The Natchez were known as mound builders. They constructed large mounds that were the center of their religious ceremonies. Natchez chiefs lived at the centers of the mounds. One of the primary mounds was built at Grand Village, near present-day Natchez, Mississippi. Another nearby mound was called Emerald Mound. The Natchez farms surrounded Grand Village and other important mounds. The tribe had several encounters with the French over the years, but eventually they lived alongside each other, as a small French settlement grew around the Natchez area. Conflict, however, and changing alliances would cost the French their friendship in the years ahead.

The Native American population throughout the colonies was greatly reduced by disease, including deadly smallpox, brought over by European explorers and settlers throughout the 16th and 17th centuries.

THE CHOCTAW

Perhaps the largest tribe in Louisiana was the Choctaw. Its population was about 22,000. La Salle encountered the Choctaw during his journey along the Mississippi River. These Indians were friendly with the English and traded furs in return for valuable goods like pots, pans, and knives.

The French explorers tried to make peace with the Choctaw, but warriors fired arrows at the white explorers from the riverbank. La Salle and his men quickly paddled away. They were intercepted by the Choctaw on the return trip up the Mississippi River in 1683. This time,

La Salle and his men fired their guns at the Indians and destroyed some of their canoes. The skirmish was minor, but the Choctaw and the French remained enemies for years to come.

The Choctaw carried on a way of life that was centuries old. Archaeologists have found an ancient mound in present-day Mississippi that may have been built by the Choctaw as early as 500 B.C. The Choctaw were farmers. Men, women, and children grew corn and other crops, such as beans, peas, pumpkins, and squash.

Among the social events that the Choctaw enjoyed were village dances and sports. Every year, the Choctaw held a corn dance to celebrate the late summer harvest time. After the corn was picked, women prepared a variety of dishes from it, including bunaha. The favorite sport of the Choctaw was ishtaboli, played by two large teams of as many as 100 players. Each player carried two rackets and tried to hit a leather ball into the goal of the opposing team.

bunaha—a Choctaw dish consisting of cornmeal and beans

ishtaboli—a Choctaw game similar to lacrosse

Choctaw houses were made from wood, bound together with vines and covered with mud. The villages were grouped together into three divisions—the northwest, the northeast, and the south. A mingo was in charge of each division. Major decisions were made by the chief and his tribal council. The council consisted of village heads and elders.

mingo—a Choctaw chief

THE CHICKASAW

Another tribe that the French hoped to make friends with was the Chickasaw. French explorers believed that an alliance with the Chickasaw tribe might help them defeat the more numerous Choctaw and lay claim to some of their territory. A permanent alliance, however, would prove to be unobtainable, as fighting with other Indian tribes and the need for self-preservation would shift the Chickasaw's loyalties between European empires.

HOMES *of the* CHICKASAW

THE CHICKASAW HAD TWO homes—one for the hot summers and another for the cooler winters. The winter home was round, made from pine poles, and covered with dry grass and clay. The summer home was an open, rectangular structure with a roof of grass that allowed the wind to blow in fresh air.

In the 17th century, the Chickasaw had a population of about 5,000 people. These Native Americans were hunters and farmers who carved out small plots from the woodlands. They grew corn and other vegetables.

Throughout the year, Chickasaw men hunted and fished along the waters of the Mississippi and neighboring rivers. Their boats, called pirogues, were made by taking down large

pirogue—a canoe made from a hollowed tree trunk

trees and burning out the insides. Hunters used bows and arrows to kill deer, which provided food and clothing. Men wore shirts and waistcloths, while women wore deerskin dresses. Deerskin was also used to make moccasins.

The Chickasaw were governed by a chief and a tribal council. Meetings of the chief and his council were attended by Indians from the local villages. They listened to the council make important laws. These laws dealt with such things as building defenses and maintaining special structures to store grain for the winter.

The alliances between Indian tribes and the European empires who hoped to amass territory in the New World shifted over the years. These friendships were often based on which French leaders were in control of the region at the time and how they treated the natives. The tribes, also hoping to advance their own interests, favored whoever had more desirable goods to trade and whoever was stronger militarily. These constantly changing loyalties were one of the biggest reasons the Louisiana colony took so long to become stable and prosperous. Eventually, the fear of losing their homelands when war broke out between France and Britain for control of North America forced the Natchez, Choctaw, and Chickasaw to declare allegiance to one or the other of these European powers. ✄

colony—a settlement that is controlled by a distant country

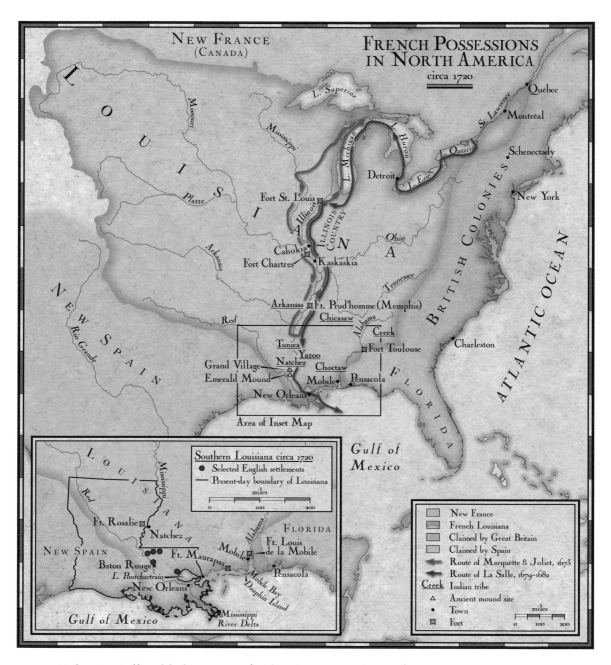

When La Salle added Louisiana (outlined in tan on the map) to New France in 1682,
he gave France control of a vast new area and the opportunity to expand its fur-trading
empire. Few people settled in Louisiana's northern Illinois Country, preferring, instead,
the area from Natchez south to New Orleans and east to Mobile (see inset map).
It is this area that will be the main focus of this book.

CHAPTER TWO

Two Brothers Guide Early Louisiana

PIERRE LE MOYNE, SIEUR D'IBERVILLE, *and his brother Jean-Baptiste Le Moyne, Sieur de Bienville, build the first French settlements in Louisiana.*

 nce La Salle claimed Louisiana for France, the French needed to bring colonists to establish settlements in the area. Otherwise, they might lose the territory, as well as the lucrative fur trade, to the English and Spanish. Some English settlements had already been established along the Mississippi River, in the area

OPPOSITE: This 1777 engraving shows Indians exchanging pelts with French fur traders. When La Salle claimed Louisiana for France, he insured that the French would have a stake in the valuable fur trade along many of the major waterways in North America.

claimed by France as part of Louisiana. This made the French very uneasy. They also had concerns that the Spanish, who already controlled Mexico to the southwest and Florida to the east might want to expand their empire into Louisiana.

On October 28, 1698, about 200 settlers and soldiers sailed in two frigates from Brest, on the coast of France. Their mission was to establish the first settlement in Louisiana. The frigates, the *Badine* and the *Marin,* were three-masted ships about 110 feet (33 m) long. They also carried cannon for protection and a cargo of cattle, pigs, and other supplies to feed the settlers. The entire expedition was under the command of Pierre Le Moyne, Sieur d'Iberville.

The 39-year-old Iberville had been born in New France. In 1690, he had fought against the English, who had established colonies in the eastern part of the region. The British claims to land in New France and the struggle for power between the two nations was an ongoing battle.

SAILING TO THE MISSISSIPPI RIVER

Iberville's ships sailed across the Atlantic Ocean to the Caribbean. There, they stopped at Santo Domingo, a Spanish settlement on the island of Hispaniola, and bought supplies. Then the French ships headed north, sailing along the west coast of Florida.

IBERVILLE'S JOURNAL

DURING HIS EXPLORATIONS OF LOUISIANA, IBERVILLE KEPT a journal. On February 14, 1699, he reported that he saw several Indians in canoes. The French explorers jumped into their own canoe to follow. The Indians headed for land. *"All the Indians fled into the woods, leaving their canoes and baggage,"* Iberville wrote.

Iberville continued to explore the area for the rest of February and then headed westward. On March 2, when he and his men were traveling in long, flat boats during a heavy storm, Iberville saw some huge rocks just ahead of him. He wrote, *"When drawing near to the rocks to take shelter, I became aware that there was a river. I passed between two of the rocks in 12 feet [3.6 m] of water, the seas quite heavy. When I got close to the rocks, I found fresh water with a very strong current."* Iberville knew that he had reached the Mississippi River.

At the end of January 1699, Iberville anchored outside Mobile Bay, in the present-day state of Alabama, which was part of the Louisiana colony. Traveling with the French commander was his brother, 18-year-old Jean-Baptiste Le Moyne, Sieur de Bienville. Iberville, his brother, and a few men paddled small boats across the treacherous sandbars at the entrance to Mobile Bay in order to explore the mainland. At one point, Iberville climbed a tree to get a view of the countryside. What he saw was miles of flat marshland covered with high pines, as well as oak and elm trees. Leaving his ships at Mobile Bay, Iberville traveled on foot westward along the coast of the Gulf of Mexico. Eventually, he reached the mouth of the Mississippi River, where La Salle had also explored seventeen years earlier in 1682.

In this painting, Pierre Le Moyne, Sieur d'Iberville, discovers the location that had been marked with the French coat of arms by La Salle when he had explored the area 17 years earlier.

During the month of March, Iberville and his brother journeyed northward along the Mississippi River, but supplies soon ran low. They turned the expedition around and headed south, back to the mouth of the Mississippi. Along the way, Iberville realized that, in order to protect the area from the Spanish or English, he needed to build a fort and establish a settlement as soon as possible. Iberville discovered a harbor along the coast of Biloxi Bay, in the present state of Mississippi. He established a fort there in April 1699. Named Fort Maurepas, it was protected by wooden walls cut from nearby forests. The French brought several cannon, which they placed on high platforms inside the fort to defend it. Iberville left some of his soldiers at the fort and returned to Mobile. From there he traveled to France to obtain more supplies. He also hoped to bring back more French settlers to begin building homes around Fort Maurepas.

BIENVILLE AND IBERVILLE

While Iberville was in France, his brother, Bienville, continued to explore the area around Fort Maurepas. He headed west with some of his men toward a large lake near the Mississippi River. The lake had been named Lake Pontchartrain by Iberville during his first expedition along the river.

Bienville had an unusual ability to learn Indian languages. He talked to Native Americans who lived along the Mississippi River and learned that the English and the Chickasaw had led an attack against a nearby Indian village. At the time, the English and Chickasaw were allied against the French. The attacks were meant to be a show of power by the English.

While Bienville was involved in his explorations, the French soldiers at Fort Maurepas were suffering. They refused to grow any food for themselves, believing that farming was beneath them. Instead, the soldiers wanted to hunt wild animals for furs, as the settlers did in New France. Some also hoped to find gold or silver in Louisiana. The French knew that the Spanish had found gold among the Indians in Mexico. Since the French had not planted any crops, they had to rely heavily on nearby Indian villages for food. Their dependency on the Indians for survival would help the French in establishing close relations with some natives as a defense against the English.

A portrait of Pierre Le Moyne, Sieur d'Iberville, commander of the 1698 mission to establish the first French settlement in Louisiana

In January 1700, Iberville returned from France with supplies for those living at Fort Maurepas. His brother probably told Iberville that a few months earlier he had prevented an English ship sailing on the Mississippi River from anchoring and exploring the region. This made Iberville realize that another post was necessary in Louisiana to guard it against the English.

IBERVILLE'S FINAL VOYAGE

After spending the spring in Louisiana, Iberville returned to France. He spent more than a year there, gathering supplies. In March 1702, he came back to Fort Maurepas ready to establish another fort in the region. Iberville had convinced the French king that a single fort would not keep the English out of Louisiana. The new post, called Fort Louis de la Mobile, was located near the present-day city of Mobile, Alabama. Under the direction of Bienville, the new fort was built to hold 24 cannon.

While Iberville was staying at Fort Louis de la Mobile, Tonti arrived in Louisiana once again. With him were Choctaw and Chickasaw chiefs. The two Indian nations had been fighting each other for more than a decade. The Chickasaw said that traders from the English settlements in the Carolinas had given their warriors guns. The English traders wanted the Chickasaw to attack the Choctaw and carry off Choctaw slaves to be used on the English plantations in the Carolinas. During these battles, the Chickasaw said that *more than 800 men [were] slain on various war parties.* Iberville and Bienville persuaded the chiefs from both tribes to sign a peace treaty with the French. The French realized that the Louisiana colony was defenseless in the event of an Indian war. The fighting would inevitably spill over into the white settlements. In addition, forming an alliance, however, temporary, might help the French if the English were to move onto their land. As an incentive, the French promised to provide the Native Americans with trading goods in exchange for furs. Then Iberville gave the chiefs numerous gifts, including bullets, guns, axes, and knives.

Iberville went back to France in April 1702. He planned to make more trips to Louisiana. He became ill, however, and died before ever reaching Louisiana again.

LOUISIANA UNDER BIENVILLE

Following the death of his brother, Bienville was appointed by the French government as the governor of Louisiana. The colony struggled to survive. By 1708, there were only about 300 people living in the French settlements. Almost half of them were French soldiers. Most of

Jean-Baptiste Le Moyne, Sieur de Bienville, brother of Iberville, was appointed governor of Louisiana in 1706 after Iberville's death.

the settlers lived by eating acorns and a little corn. They raised a few farm animals, such as pigs, goats, and chickens.

At this time, all the settlers in the Louisiana colony were men. Bienville wanted to bring women to the colony.

The French government hoped that women would help increase the number of settlers by marrying the French colonists and having families. The government also hoped that families would settle down on farms and begin growing crops to feed themselves. Very few women, however, wanted to leave France for the wilderness in Louisiana. Eventually, the government persuaded about 20 women to sail from France to Louisiana by promising them husbands. After they arrived in Mobile, the women did not like the food and found the men very unattractive. Historians think that most of them returned to France.

In 1711, Bienville's headquarters at Mobile Bay was struck by a terrible flood. He asked the king for more money to construct a new fort at Mobile and for additional soldiers to defend it. So far, King Louis XIV had not seen any profit from the Louisiana colony. The French had found no gold and very little fur trading was being conducted in the colony. The Chickasaw were trading with the English and refused to trade with the French. (In the treaty brokered earlier by Bienville and his brother, the Indians were not limited to trading only with the French, so they could shift their loyalty to whoever had what they needed to trade for at the time.) The English supplied them with better trading goods, such as kettles and knives. The French government did not have enough money to build a new fort for Bienville or properly defend Louisiana. In order to cut expenses, the king decided to turn the colony over to a private company.

CHAPTER THREE

Two Companies Run the Colony

FOR TWO DECADES, LOUISIANA IS RUN *by two French companies. One is owned by Antoine Crozat. The other is called the Mississippi Company. New Orleans becomes the capital of the colony.*

n 1712, King Louis XIV turned the management of his colony of Louisiana over to a wealthy French merchant and banker named Antoine Crozat.

The king gave Crozat a 15-year contract in Louisiana. Crozat's company was permitted to keep the profits from any

OPPOSITE: Bienville, a surveyor at his side, looks over plans in preparation for building on the site for the city of New Orleans.

trade in furs or animal skins in Louisiana. (By the early 18th century, the main export from Louisiana to Europe was deerskin, used for clothing.) The company, however, had to pay the king 25 percent of all money earned from any gold mines that might be discovered there. Crozat was also in charge of bringing new settlers to Louisiana and paying for their transportation. He paid for presents to the Indians to keep them from becoming English allies and destroying the colony. Although Crozat ran Louisiana, it still remained a colony of France under the authority of the French government.

SIEUR DE CADILLAC IN LOUISIANA

The French government appointed Antoine de La Mothe, Sieur de Cadillac, as governor of Louisiana. On June 5, 1713, Cadillac landed at Dauphin Island in Mobile Bay. From the time he arrived in the colony, he never liked it. He wrote that Louisiana was *a wretched country, good for nothing, and incapable of producing either tobacco, wheat, or vegetables."* A short time later he wrote: "*According to the proverb, 'Bad country, bad people,' one can say that they are a heap of the dregs of Canada . . . a cut-throat set . . . with no respect for religion."* Cadillac hoped to get rich by discovering gold in Louisiana. Indeed, he used money given to him by Crozat to search for mines. Crozat, however, wanted the new governor to use the money to set up trading posts with the Indians. The Indians would bring in additional skins and furs that the company could sell in Europe.

When Crozat and Cadillac took over the running of Louisiana, there were just over 300 settlers in the colony. Crozat had been given control of trade in Louisiana. To make money, Crozat tried to drive a hard bargain with the coureurs de bois, French traders who lived among the Indians. In fact, he paid as little as possible for furs and deerskins. Eager to make money, Crozat neglected his other responsibilities as manager of the colony. He brought very few additional settlers to Louisiana. No gold mines were discovered, no new towns were built, and the colony continued to struggle.

coureurs de bois— French fur traders in early North America

BIENVILLE AND CADILLAC

In 1714, Louisiana was threatened by a powerful tribe of Native Americans called the Creek. The Creek lived in Alabama and Georgia, and were strong allies of the English.

Although Bienville was no longer governor of Louisiana, he was still respected for his knowledge of the Native Americans. In April, Governor Cadillac sent Bienville northward from Mobile with a small army of French soldiers and Choctaw Indians. His expedition sailed up the Alabama River in two small ships. Bienville met with various small tribes of Indians living along the river and distributed presents to their chiefs. He hoped to make allies of these groups in order to increase French strength in the event of an attack by the Creek. Near the present-day site of Tuskegee, Alabama, Bienville decided to establish a new French post, which he called Fort Toulouse. Its purpose was to demonstrate French power to the Indians so they would remain peaceful. Leaving about 30 soldiers and eight cannon at the fort, Bienville returned to Mobile.

The French now had settlements at Fort Toulouse, Mobile, and Fort Maurepas. These were the first in the chain the French hoped would link Louisiana to the rest of New France and prevent British settlements from spreading westward. The French also hoped that the forts would demonstrate the empire's strength to the natives living in the region.

Bienville and Cadillac did not get along well. At this time, historians believe, Cadillac decided to send Bienville on a campaign against the Natchez Indians, hoping that Bienville might be killed. The Natchez lived in the present-day state of Mississippi. In 1715, they had burned a trading post and killed French traders on the Mississippi River. The hostility of this group of Native Americans threatened French fur-trading activities.

Bienville wanted at least 80 soldiers to march against the Natchez, but Cadillac provided him with less than half that number. Bienville headed northward in the spring of 1716, stopping at an island in the Mississippi River where he began building a new fort. Eventually, several Natchez chiefs arrived at the island to investigate what the French were doing. Catching them off guard, Bienville ordered his men to tie up the chiefs and hold them as prisoners. Bienville told them that they must pay for the deaths of the French traders by ordering the murderers to be killed. Several days later, a Natchez chief brought in the heads of the three Indians accused of the murders. The Natchez also signed a peace treaty with Bienville and assisted him in building the new fort. Fort Rosalie was established on the present-day site of Natchez, Mississippi.

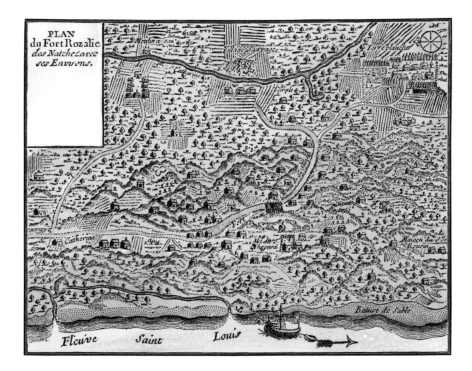

Fort Rosalie (or Rozalie), which stands on the site of present-day Natchez, Mississippi, was built by Bienville with help from the Natchez Indians with whom he was able to negotiate a peace treaty. The Mississippi River (Fleuve Saint Louis) runs north-south along the bottom edge of the map.

THE MISSISSIPPI COMPANY

Soon after Bienville returned to Mobile, he was asked by the French government to replace Cadillac as the governor of the colony. Cadillac was fired because he had stirred up trouble with the Natchez and spent much of his time looking in vain for gold mines instead of governing the colony. The colony had not grown under Cadillac, and Bienville was recognized for the hard work he had done keeping peace with the Indians. Bienville served as governor from 1717 to 1725. During this time, Crozat gave up management of Louisiana because he was unable to make any money there. The French government decided to make an arrangement with a successful financier named John Law that was similar to its agreement with Crozat.

John Law was given permission by the French government in 1717 to organize the Company of the West (also known as the Company of the Indies), later known as the Mississippi Company. The new company was given control of the fur trade and any mines discovered in Louisiana. The company was also given much of the land in Louisiana. Nevertheless, Louisiana would still be considered a royal colony.

Law never traveled to Louisiana. In France, he published pamphlets to persuade colonists to leave Europe and move to the colony. The pamphlets described rich gold and silver mines in Louisiana. They also claimed that the colony's soil could grow all kinds of crops—from apples to wheat. People in Europe had no way of knowing that this information was false. As a result of these advertisements, some people invested in the Mississippi Company. Others sailed to the colony from Germany and Switzerland. To gain more settlers from France, however, Law was forced to ask the French government to release criminals from jail and send them to Louisiana.

This 1720 poster of Native Americans trading with the French at the mouth of the Mississippi was distributed by John Law's Mississippi Company to promote emigration to the Louisiana colony.

From 1717 to 1721, about 7,000 settlers arrived in the colony. Among them were prisoners who had been con-victed of smuggling and other crimes. Frenchman Pierre

Voisin, for example, was a smuggler, and Claude du Val was an army deserter. The settlers also included about 2,500 indentured servants, known as engagés. In return for their passage to Louisiana, they were required to work for three or more years, farming the lands owned by the Mississippi Company.

engagés—indentured servants in Louisiana who were required to work for three or more years on the lands owned by the Mississippi Company in return for paid passage to the colony

The new settlers sent by Law arrived at Mobile Bay. Some were taken to the town of Natchez, while others traveled to Illinois Country. Many colonists went to Bienville's new settlement at New Orleans. Bienville had established New Orleans in 1718. The site lay at a bend in the Mississippi River, not far from Lake Pontchartrain. Bienville understood that creating a settlement on this strategic site would give the French an enormous amount of control of the trade and goods shipped along the river. Some of the prisoners brought to Louisiana were taken there to help build the settlement. They battled alligators, snakes, and mosquitoes to carve out the town. Levees, or dikes, were put up to keep the Mississippi River from washing into New Orleans. The workers built small cabins out of cypress logs for the settlers, as well as a hospital and a church for Capuchin priests.

The Capuchins were a group of Catholic clergymen. They came to Louisiana to provide religious services for the settlers and to convert the Indians to Christianity. They were successful in winning some converts and providing spiritual help to the settlers in Louisiana. In 1725, Father Raphael de Luxembourg set up a Capuchin school for boys on St. Ann Street in New Orleans—the first school in Louisiana.

Despite the work of the new settlers in Louisiana, the colony still struggled. Dampness caused some of the furs that they trapped or purchased from the Native Americans to rot. Wheat would not grow in Louisiana because the climate was too hot and humid. The settlers relied on shipments of supplies sent from France. Wheat also came from French settlements located in Illinois Country. But these supplies were not always enough to prevent widespread starvation.

Colonists sent to Louisiana in 1720 by John Law lived in this camp, or settlement, near Biloxi Bay, along the coast.

Louisiana's FIRST HISTORIAN

AMONG THE SETTLERS WHO CAME TO LOUISIANA WAS Antoine le Page du Pratz, a well-to-do gentleman from France. Du Pratz later published a history of the French colony, which provided one of the only early eyewitness accounts of New Orleans. Du Pratz landed at Dauphin Island in Mobile Bay in August 1718. He spent four months on the island before he could find a boat to take him up the Mississippi River to New Orleans. When he arrived, the construction of the new town was just beginning. *"At that moment all that there was of New Orleans was a shed covered with dry branches, where the commandant [Bienville] lodged,"* he wrote. Du Pratz found a settler who *"lodged me in a cabin. . . . He gave other cabins to my workmen and we were pleased to get ourselves under shelter so promptly in a wild country."*

WAR WITH SPAIN

While the settlers struggled with starvation, a war broke out with Spain in 1719, which spilled over into North America. Bienville decided to lead an expedition against the Spanish town of Pensacola, in Spanish Florida, near the border of French Louisiana. Pensacola was a thriving Spanish settlement in western Florida, and the French believed that it threatened the future of Louisiana. With the help of his brother Chateaugne, Bienville took an army of soldiers and Indians eastward. The expedition included four ships commanded by another of Bienville's brothers, Serigny. In May, they launched an attack on Pensacola from land and sea, forcing the town to surrender.

After the battle, Chateaugne remained in charge of Pensacola. He was soon attacked by a large Spanish force that retook the town. In August 1719, the Spanish attacked the French colony at Mobile. The town was fiercely defended by Serigny, and the Spanish were forced to retreat to Pensacola. The war soon ended, but relations and borders between the Spanish and French colonies remained shaky.

When John Law's Mississippi Company went bankrupt, settlers who had been deceived by promises of opportunity in Louisiana took to the streets of France in protest and anger.

Back in France, those who had invested in the Mississippi Company began to realize that there was no silver and gold in Louisiana. The stock they had bought in the company gradually lost its value. The Mississippi Company went bankrupt in 1720, and John Law fled from France to escape angry share-holders. The growth and bank-ruptcy of the company was known as the Mississippi Bubble. Nevertheless, the Mississippi Company managed to scrape together some money and continued running Louisiana until 1731.

THE FAMINE OF 1719 — 1721

JEAN FRANCOIS BENJAMIN DUMONT, A SOLDIER IN Louisiana, described the difficulties faced by the new Louisiana settlers. One of these hardships was famine, because the Louisiana settlers could not grow enough food to feed themselves. The hot, humid climate made growing wheat and corn almost impossible, because the crops rotted in the wet weather. As Dumont wrote:

Although great care was taken in France to send abundantly provisions of every kind to the colony, yet all their care could not prevent want being felt there. It was so great that the commandant was obliged to send soldiers, workmen, and even officers, to the nearest Indians of the country . . . who received them . . . with good hominy [corn] boiled with good store of meat or bear oil. . . . At last, the famine was so severe that a great number died, some from eating herbs . . . which, instead of prolonging life, produced death.

THE GROWTH OF LOUISIANA

In Europe, most people lost interest in Louisiana. Important changes, however, were occurring in the colony itself. The Germans and Swiss who had come to Louisiana established farms along the Mississippi River. Unlike the French, who were interested in fur trading, the Swiss and Germans grew vegetables and raised cattle. There were still more men than women in the colony, so some ended up marrying Native Americans. As the two cultures merged, the families resulting from those unions began farming and learning how to sustain themselves along the Mississippi frontier.

In 1722, Bienville received permission to move the capital of Louisiana from Mobile to New Orleans. New Orleans was more centrally located in the colony and protected the important trading area along the Mississippi River. On September 11, however, New Orleans was struck by a powerful hurricane that wiped out many of the buildings. The settlers immediately began to rebuild. The effort was led by Bienville and two French engineers, Chevalier Le Blond de la Tour and Adrien de Pauger. They laid out the streets of the town at right angles. Along the river was a large square, called the Place d'Armes. A sawmill was put up to cut logs for building houses, including a home for Bienville on the Place d'Armes. Each house was a single story high with a bark roof and windows covered with linen to let in light. The houses were raised up on blocks, because New Orleans was on the same level as the Mississippi River. The town was rebuilt in a way that was far better than it had been before the hurricane struck.

This engraving shows young Frenchwomen making their good byes as they board a ship departing France in the late 1720s for New Orleans, the new capital of French Louisiana.

In 1728, young women began to arrive in New Orleans from France. They came from orphanages and jails. The girls lived with a group of nuns in New Orleans until they were married. Ursuline nuns opened a school for young girls, both white and Native American. The nuns were part of an effort by the Catholic Church to convert the Indians to Christianity. This is considered the oldest school for girls in the present-day United States. The girls learned to read, they were taught the Catholic religion, and some of them learned to be nurses. Among the Ursuline nuns was Sister Madeleine Hachard. She had traveled from France through a terrible storm on the Atlantic Ocean and eventually arrived in New Orleans. She described the city this way:

> *The city itself is very handsome and regularly built. The houses are well constructed of wood, plastered, whitewashed . . . and open to the light. The roofs of the houses are covered with shingles. . . . Suffice to say, they sing here a song in the streets to the effect that this town is as fine a sight as Paris.*

New Orleans was still a tiny frontier town compared to Paris, but it was growing. By the 1720s, the population of New Orleans had reached more than 500 settlers. During the 1720s, the colony also began importing slaves from Africa. Slavery would change the future of Louisiana.

CHAPTER FOUR

Africans in Louisiana

THE MISSISSIPPI COMPANY *brings slaves from Africa and introduces two new crops—indigo and rice— that transform life in the colony.*

 hile the Mississippi Company ran Louisiana (1718–1731), about 6,000 African slaves were brought to the colony. Most of them came from an area on the west coast of Africa known as Senegambia. This territory is located in the modern West African countries of Senegal, Gambia and parts of Mali. The French had established slave-trading posts there.

Africans living in this area had developed very successful cultures. On their farms, they grew a variety of

OPPOSITE: A European slave merchant bargains for two young Africans with a local slave trader on Goreé Island off the coast of Senegal in Africa.

crops, including rice, corn, cotton, and indigo. Many of these crops would eventually be grown in Louisiana. In addition to being excellent farmers, many of these people were skilled artisans. They worked as blacksmiths and also made fine gold and silver jewelry. Weavers created beautiful clothing from the cotton growing in nearby fields.

AFRICAN CRAFTSMEN

JEAN BAPTISTE LABAT WORKED FOR A FRENCH TRADING company in Senegambia during the 18th century. He wrote that the African craftsmen there had a variety of skills that enabled them to work as blacksmiths and goldsmiths:

In a word, they unite in one single person all the workers who use hammer and anvil. . . . Their tools only consist of a very small anvil, a goatskin bellows [to keep a fire hot], a few hammers, tongs, and two or three files [to shape the hot metal into finished items]. . . . They never tire of making fairly delicate works of gold or silver.

These works included bracelets, necklaces, and ornate handles for swords.

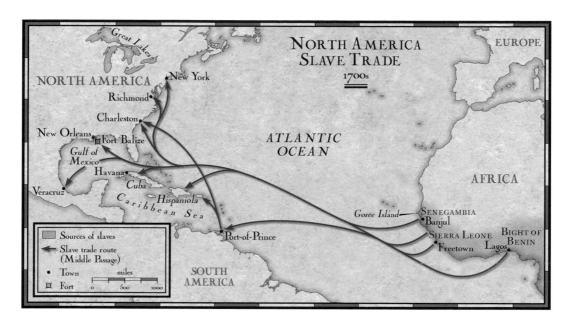

The Middle Passage took slaves from the west coast of Africa to ports along the coast of North America. Not shown are the routes that took millions more slaves from these and other areas of Africa to South America, especially Brazil.

AFRICAN SLAVE TRADERS AND THE EUROPEANS

From 1719 to 1731, 23 French ships took slaves from West Africa to New Orleans. Slaves were kept in chains during the journey, which often lasted about six months. Along the way, some of the slaves died of diseases, such as smallpox, that spread rapidly in the crowded conditions. For example, the ship *Diane* started out with 516 slaves but reached Louisiana with only 464. Slaves also died from dysentery and scurvy.

scurvy—a disease in which severe bleeding under the skin and of the gums is caused by a lack of vitamin C

Once the slave ships arrived in Louisiana, the Africans were unloaded at Fort Balize. This French post was built at the mouth of the Mississippi River. Some of these slaves worked on lands belonging to the Mississippi Company. Others were auctioned off to farmers in Illinois Country who grew wheat and wanted slaves to help them till the fields and harvest the grain. Many slaves were sent to New Orleans. Here, they were put to work erecting new buildings or building levees to protect the new town from being flooded.

Some slaves escaped and hid in the swamps with other runaways. The French called these fugitives maroons. Some of these people managed to take food, guns, and ammunition with them. They survived by hunting, fishing, and trapping animals. Gradually, they might be joined by more runaways and set up a small community in the swamps. Since the swamps were dangerous, owners rarely went there to find their escaped slaves.

MOLURON

AFRICANS ADMIRED THOSE SLAVES who escaped. One of their heroes was Moluron. He continually ran away from his master but was always caught. Africans sang a folk song about Moluron.

Moluron! He! Moluron! He!
It's not today I'm in the world.
If you treat me well, I'll stay.
If you treat me bad, I'll escape.

The Skills of the Africans

The African slaves who were brought to Louisiana had many valuable skills. In addition to transporting human cargo, slave traders brought rice seeds from Africa to the New World. With the Africans' knowledge and experience with growing rice, this grain became an important crop in the colony.

The Africans also knew how to grow indigo and produce the beautiful dye that came from the plant. Blue indigo dye was highly valued by kings and other members of Europe's nobility for making the royal blue robes they wore. Harvesting and processing indigo was a difficult and dirty task. The plants were soaked in huge vats of water until they rotted. The smell was terrible, and the vats were infested with swarms of flies. Without slaves to do this work, white planters would not have been able to produce so much of this dye.

Slaves soak indigo plants in bug-infested vats of water while others harvest the plants that produce the valuable blue dye.

In addition to contributing their agricultural skills, African slaves worked as blacksmiths in Louisiana. Some also served as assistants to French craftsmen, learning how to be locksmiths, carpenters, and shipbuilders. Slaves were put to work on boats that carried goods up and down the Mississippi River. The French had established settlements in Illinois Country at Kaskaskia, Cahokia, and Fort Chartres along the Mississippi River. Wheat grown in Illinois Country, where the climate was drier, was shipped downriver to feed the colonists in southern Louisiana.

LOUISIANA PLANTATIONS

Slaves on plantations were forced by their white masters to work long hours. Often, the slaves were not given enough to eat. Indeed, one observer called them *walking skeletons.* A report from the Mississippi Company indicated that their food was often rotten. In 1725, the company decided to increase the usual meal for slaves on its plantations from 1 pound (0.45 kg) of corn a day per slave to 1.5 pounds (0.7 kg).

Slaves worked and lived on plantations that were long, ribbon-like strips of land laid out along the Mississippi River. The plantation houses were one-story buildings built of cypress wood. Some of them had furs on the floors for carpets. Near the plantation houses, the slaves lived in simple cabins with dirt floors and a fireplace for heating and cooking.

During the 1720s, a small number of planters owned most of the slaves. Around Natchez, a few planters had begun growing tobacco. They owned about 900 slaves. On 50 other plantations, more than 1,000 slaves were put to work growing rice, tobacco, and indigo. Colonists without slaves worked small farms, traded with the Indians, or worked as artisans.

CODE NOIR

THE CODE NOIR, OR BLACK CODE, DESCRIBED THE WAY that masters were supposed to treat African slaves. Established by the French in Louisiana in 1724, the code required that *"all slaves in the province [of Louisiana] be instructed and baptized in the Catholic religion."* Slaves were also supposed to be given a day off on Sundays and holidays.

Plantation owners were afraid that if slaves met together, they might plan a revolt. Therefore, the code did not allow *"slaves belonging to different masters to assemble in crowds, by day or by night . . . either at one of their masters or elsewhere . . . .* [Slaves were forbidden] *to carry offensive Weapons or heavy sticks, under penalty of the whip."*

The code also tried to give slaves some protection from harsh masters. The slaves were permitted to work for themselves one day per week, growing their own food. Slaves were also encouraged to report masters who did not clothe or feed them properly. In addition, masters were expected to care for sick and old slaves.

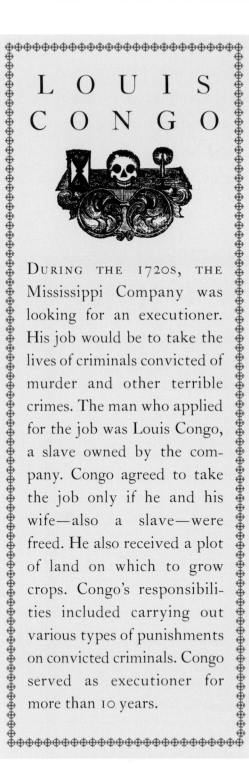

LOUIS CONGO

DURING THE 1720S, THE Mississippi Company was looking for an executioner. His job would be to take the lives of criminals convicted of murder and other terrible crimes. The man who applied for the job was Louis Congo, a slave owned by the company. Congo agreed to take the job only if he and his wife—also a slave—were freed. He also received a plot of land on which to grow crops. Congo's responsibilities included carrying out various types of punishments on convicted criminals. Congo served as executioner for more than 10 years.

FAMILY LIFE AND CULTURE

Slaves held onto many of the traditions that they had in Africa. The Code Noir required that slaves become Catholics, but they continued to follow African religious beliefs. They also kept their African names. French masters might give their slaves names like "Claude," but the Africans called themselves by their original names, such as "Baraca," "Matha," and "Gros."

Families were the center of life among slaves in Louisiana. Slaves in New Orleans or on the plantations married and raised children. The Code Noir prevented these children from being sold away from their parents before the age of 14. These children grew up among large extended families. Some of the girls were educated by the Ursuline nuns.

A few slaves succeeded in purchasing their freedom. Some of them saved money from growing their own vegetables and selling them. Others were permitted to keep some of the money they earned as artisans. Still others had their freedom purchased by blacks who had already become free. In addition, some slaves were freed by their masters after long service. Bienville, for example, freed his slave, Jorge, and Jorge's wife, Marie, after 26 years.

During the 18th century, Africans began to intermarry with Native Americans or with white settlers. The children of these marriages and their descendants became known as Creoles, and created a new and distinct culture in Louisiana. Some Creoles were free blacks, but the majority remained slaves. Creoles developed a distinctive language that combined French with African words. For example, their name for a thick seafood stew was "gumbo." "Gumbo" is an African word for okra, a vegetable that is an ingredient in the stew.

Creole—anyone born in Louisiana who was at least part African American

Slave women are watched over by an overseer to ensure that the master gets maximum effort out of his human property.

VIOLENCE IN LOUISIANA

For most Africans, daily life in Louisiana was very harsh. The Code Noir did not protect them from being whipped and beaten. This harsh treatment made them go to great lengths to obtain their freedom.

THE REVOLT OF 1731

LOUISIANA BARELY AVOIDED A SLAVE REVOLT IN 1731. The conspiracy was betrayed by a female slave working in New Orleans. At night, French officials went to a plantation where the conspirators were meeting. Outside one of the cabins, they listened as the slaves inside planned their revolt. One of the leaders turned out to be a trusted slave named Samba who worked for the Mississippi Company.

The following night, the French officials returned and listened as other conspirators plotted the revolt. Soon afterward, the French arrested all the slaves. They were questioned, found guilty, and executed.

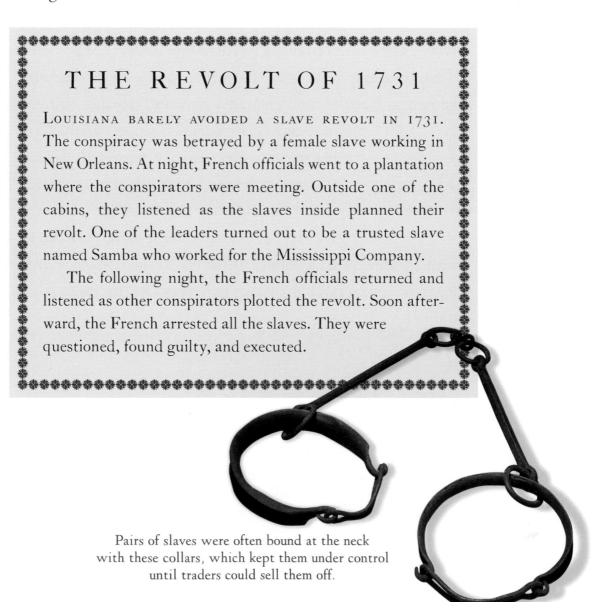

Pairs of slaves were often bound at the neck with these collars, which kept them under control until traders could sell them off.

Things weren't much better for Native Americans. In 1729, the French commander of the post at Natchez ordered the Indians to leave their village at White Apple. The French wanted to establish more tobacco plantations in the area. Rumors spread that the French Army planned to wipe out the Natchez tribe. The Native Americans met in their villages and decided to strike before the French did. They received support from many African-American slaves working on the tobacco plantations around Natchez. The slaves believed that a victory over the French would win them their freedom.

On the day of the attack, November 28, 1729, Natchez warriors traveled to the homes of the French settlers around Fort Rosalie. The Native Americans promised to bring the settlers food in return for permission to use French guns to hunt deer and other animals. The settlers agreed to the trade. As soon as the Indians took the weapons, they began murdering the settlers. More than half of the white population of 430 settlers was killed.

Louisiana governor Étienne de Périer, who had replaced Bienville in 1726, gathered a force of settlers and Choctaw Indians to fight the Natchez. They were joined by 15 black slaves who were eventually freed for helping the French. For the next two years, the French and their allies fought the Natchez. Many Natchez warriors were killed. Finally, the Natchez were overwhelmed and almost completely destroyed. ✺

CHAPTER FIVE

Struggles of a Small Royal Colony

DURING THE 1730S AND 1740S, *Louisiana grows under the governorships of Bienville and Pierre de Rigaud de Vaudreuil.*

 till unable to make enough money in Louisiana to justify the expense of protecting and settling the region, the Mississippi Company handed the financial management of the colony back to the French government in 1731. Over the next 20 years, the life of the colony was shaped by two strong colonial governors, Bienville and Pierre de Rigaud de Vaudreuil.

OPPOSITE: Pierre de Rigaud de Vaudreuil (1740–1817) helped bring prosperity to the struggling Louisiana colony.

In 1732, Bienville was appointed governor of Louisiana once again. He remained in charge of the colony until 1743. By the time he left, the population of the colony stood at about 6,400 people. About 1,700 settlers were white, and approximately 4,700 were black. The settlers were scattered throughout a few small towns. The largest was New Orleans with 3,800 people, about 3,000 of whom were black. Other settlements included Fort Balize, Natchez, and Mobile. Less than 1,000 settlers lived in Illinois Country, which was governed from New Orleans by Bienville.

One of Bienville's major problems was dealing with the unstable Native American population. The French and British still competed for Indian allies. However, the British offered the Native Americans superior trading goods, including guns. As a result, British traders had a firm alliance with the powerful Chickasaw tribes. These tribes threatened the Louisiana colony during the 1730s.

The French did not have enough troops to defeat the Chickasaw. Therefore, Louisiana once again tried to make strong alliances with other Native American tribes—especially the Choctaw. In 1736, Bienville put together a small army to attack the Chickasaw. The force included about 600 white soldiers and blacks, as well as several hundred Choctaw warriors. Along the trail, however, the army was ambushed by the Chickasaw. Bienville lost about 100 men and was forced to retreat to New Orleans.

In 1739, Bienville led a much larger army—almost 1,800 soldiers—against the Chickasaw. This army was too strong for the Chickasaw to defeat, and they decided to negotiate a peace treaty with the French. However, even after this, Chickasaw war parties continued to strike at French settlements and boats along the Mississippi River.

Native Americans in Louisiana track their enemy in one of the many skirmishes between Indians and the French throughout the mid-1700s.

Meanwhile, some of the Choctaw warriors no longer supported the French. The Choctaw often spent so many weeks on raiding missions that they had little time to raise their crops. A powerful chief named Red Shoes did not like the French. He said that *for too long a time the French have been causing the blood of the Indians to be shed.* Red Shoes began meeting with the Chickasaw, hoping to create peace between the tribes. He also started assisting British traders.

In 1746, some of Red Shoes's followers killed three French traders. The French government offered a reward for Red Shoes. The following year, he was killed by a Choctaw warrior. Civil war broke out among the Choctaw. In 1750 the Choctaw who supported the British were defeated by an army sent by the French.

POLITICS
among the
CHOCTAW

FATHER MICHAEL BAUDOUIN WAS A JESUIT PRIEST WHO lived at the Choctaw village of Chickasawhay. He tried to convert some of the Indians to Christianity. While living among the Choctaw, he observed the negotiations between the French and their Indian allies. *"All the villages are so many little republics in which each one does as he likes,"* Father Baudouin wrote. There was also a Great Chief of the Choctaw who *"was given a very considerable annual present."* But he could not keep the entire gift for himself. He had to split it up with *"the principal chiefs of the different Choctaw villages."* The French then began giving presents directly to these chiefs. Father Baudouin added that *"those who receive them directly from the French concern themselves very little about the Great Chief of their nation whose power they do not fear."*

LOUISIANA UNDER GOVERNOR VAUDREUIL

In 1743, Pierre de Rigaud de Vaudreuil was named to succeed Bienville. When Vaudreuil arrived in Louisiana, the economy of the colony was beginning to improve. Sawmills around New Orleans were producing wooden boards for new homes. In addition, Louisiana produced about 500 pounds (230 kg) of pitch and tar for export abroad. These products came from pine trees. They were used to seal the spaces between boards on ships to make them watertight. Louisiana also produced 200,000 pounds (91,000 kg) of tobacco and 15,000 pounds (6,800 kg) of indigo.

During much of his term as governor, Vaudreuil struggled with the intendant of Louisiana. Together, the intendant and the governor were supposed to run the colony. During the first five years of Vaudreuil's term, the intendant was Sébastien-François-Ange Le Normant de Mézy. He constantly criticized the governor for spending too much money, especially on presents for the Native Americans. Vaudreuil believed that presents for the Indian leaders were essential, especially for the Choctaw, to keep them as allies. In a letter to the French government, Vaudreuil wrote, *"Le Normant seeks only to gain merit in your eyes by all these financial arrangements."*

intendant—a French finance official in Louisiana in charge of the colony's budget

Romance ABOARD SHIP

WHEN VAUDREUIL SAILED FOR Louisiana, he met Jeanne-Charlotte de Fleury Deschambault aboard the ship. A romance began during the voyage to Louisiana, and three years later they were married.

Madame Vaudreuil played an important role in Louisiana. She arranged many lavish parties at the governor's home to entertain important guests. Indeed, the first play written in Louisiana, *The Indian Father*, was performed at the governor's house in 1753.

Le Normant finally left Louisiana in 1748. He was replaced by Honoré Michel de Villebois de La Rouvilliere, who also criticized Vaudreuil. He accused the governor of allowing his friends to make money in illegal trading activities. The governor did allow Louisiana plantation owners to smuggle indigo to British traders. Even though this helped improve the economy of Louisiana, this activity was prohibited by the royal government because the French king did not see any of the illegal profits. In spite of these criticisms, Vaudreuil remained governor, and his policies strengthened the colony.

Governor Vaudreuil opened up trade with the Spanish colonies in Cuba and Mexico. (Spain and France were both at war with Great Britain during the 1740s.) The British Navy intercepted Spanish ships bringing supplies to Spain's colonies in America. Trade increased between these colonies and Louisiana. Fort Balize became a busy trading center.

Fort Balize, at the mouth of the Mississippi, became a busy commercial center when Governor Vaudreuil opened up trade between Louisiana and Spain's colonies in the New World.

Meanwhile, Governor Vaudreuil persuaded the French government to spend more money on Louisiana's defenses. As a result, the government sent additional soldiers and strengthened its forts in the colony. These policies helped the colonists, who supplied food to the soldiers and lumber to build new forts.

Although he was successful in Louisiana, Vaudreuil wanted to become governor of New France. His father had served as governor of Montréal, and Vaudreuil wanted to follow in his footsteps. In 1755, he was finally appointed to this position. On May 3, Vaudreuil and his wife left for Québec. 🕸

CHAPTER SIX

Illinois Country

ILLINOIS COUNTRY, A SMALL GROUP *of settlements governed from New Orleans, provides Louisiana with wheat and other important food supplies.*

he French governors of Louisiana were also in charge of settlements in Illinois Country, which included Cahokia, Kaskaskia, and Fort Chartres in the present-day state of Illinois. Cahokia was founded in 1699, Kaskaskia in 1703, and Fort Chartres in 1719.

Illinois Country was a vital link in the French empire that stretched from Canada to the mouth of the Mississippi River. Farms in this region provided Louisiana with essential food, such as wheat and corn. In addition, French forts

OPPOSITE: A coureur de bois on snowshoes journeys south of New France to Illinois Country in 1722, seeking new sources for furs.

here helped to link Canada with Louisiana and to prevent British settlers from moving westward.

Considered part of Louisiana, the settlements in Illinois were established primarily as trading posts to purchase furs from the local Native Americans. At first, there were only a few traders and French soldiers at each post. The numbers of colonists gradually increased as other traders came, settled, and raised families. In 1752, the population of Illinois Country was about 1,400 people.

Over the years, the French government sent more women to Illinois Country to marry and have children. Some of these women were the criminals and orphans who had been sent to New Orleans by the Mississippi Company. In an effort to increase the number of settlers in Illinois, the French government also sent male convicts to the colony. Unfortunately, the idea of living among convicts made the region undesirable to other people who might have emigrated there.

Immigrants from Switzerland, Germany, and Italy came to Illinois, too. Settlers would arrive in the Gulf ports of Louisiana and travel up river to Illinois. Some of the male colonists married women from local Native American tribes, such as the Pawnee and the Arikara. Some French coureurs de bois who traded with the Native Americans also married into the local tribes.

LIFE IN ILLINOIS COUNTRY

Like the farms in southern Louisiana, those in Illinois Country were laid out along the Mississippi River. They were narrow, ribbon-like pieces of property. A log house and a garden were located in front, along the river. The furniture—chairs, tables, beds, and chests of drawers—was made by the farmers themselves or by local artisans. Some houses also had glass windows with cloth curtains. Cloth and glass were imported from France through New Orleans and then transported up the Mississippi River.

A Jesuit priest preaches to a Native American in Illinois Country in hopes of converting him and members of his tribe to Christianity.

The settlers, known as habitants, enclosed their property with picket fences. Beyond the house lay fields where

habitants—French farmers in Illinois Country

settlers grew corn and wheat. By the 1740s, several hundred slaves had been transported from other parts of Louisiana to the settlements in Illinois to work in the fields. Slaves also worked at missions run by Jesuit priests in Illinois Country. These priests preached among the Native Americans, hoping to win converts to Christianity.

New Orleans, the capital of all of Louisiana, was a long distance from Illinois. The trip downriver to the Gulf took about four weeks. Usually, boatmen traveled in a pirogue or a bateau. The trip upriver against the current took even longer—three or four months. From Illinois, boatmen carried wheat, corn, and furs to New Orleans.

bateau—a French boat with oars or sails used on the Mississippi River

TRAVELING
the Mississippi River

PERRIN DU LAC, WHO LIVED ALONG THE MISSISSIPPI RIVER, described the lives of Mississippi boatmen.

No trips are more arduous than those on the Mississippi. The men who row up it are exposed to the weather, sleep on the ground, and eat nothing but maize [corn] and bacon. On long voyages . . . they suffer indescribably. They wear nothing except what is required for decency, and their skins, burned by the sun, are continuously peeling. . . . It is not unusual for them to succumb to fatigue and to die oar in hand.

Since the distance between New Orleans and Illinois was so great, many decisions were made by local governments in each community throughout the region. These community assemblies were attended by all the landowners. One important issue was setting up new pastures where all the villagers could keep their cows.

syndics—local officials in French towns in Louisiana

Each settlement had local officials called syndics. They carried on the day-to-day work of the community, such as collecting taxes. Syndics were also in charge of inspecting fences to make sure they were properly built. Fences were essential to prevent a farmer's pigs from wandering into a neighbor's fields and eating the crops. Syndics were also authorized to fine or arrest any colonist who stole a horse.

In 1754, the links in France's colonial empire were tested when a bloody war broke out between Britain and France for control of North America. ❈

CHAPTER SEVEN

French and Spanish Louisiana

FRANCE LOSES THE LOUISIANA COLONY, *which is turned over to Spain as a result of war and a secret treaty.*

eginning in 1754, New France was locked in a war with the British in North America. About the same time, a new governor, Louis Billouart de Kerlerec, arrived in New Orleans. Kerlerec, a naval captain, found that most of the French troops had been ordered to leave Louisiana and go north to Ohio Country

OPPOSITE: This 19th-century painting illustrates British soldiers using force to subdue and expel Acadians from their home in eastern New France in 1755.

and other areas of New France to fight the war. The outcome of the war between France and England changed the history of Louisiana.

THE ACADIANS AND LOUISIANA

The French and Indian War (1754–1763) was fought between France and Britain for control of North America. The war began in 1754 in the Ohio Valley, not far from where the French established an outpost called Fort Duquesne, on the site of present-day Pittsburgh, Pennsylvania. The British also claimed this region as part of Virginia. Major George Washington, fighting for Great Britain as commander of the Virginia militia, was unsuccessful in driving the French from the region. The French would not prove as victorious in the years to come.

In 1755, the British drove French settlers from an area of eastern New France called Acadia (founded in present-day Nova Scotia). The 18,000 Acadian residents had lived in this region for more than a hundred years. They had established settlements at Grand Pré, Annapolis Royal, St. John, and St. Croix. The Acadians traded with the local Native Americans for furs, fished in the waters of the Atlantic Ocean, and raised cattle. Although Great Britain had controlled Acadia since 1710, the French settlers had been allowed to remain.

The outbreak of war changed the situation. In the fall of 1755, the British governor of Acadia, Charles Lawrence, ordered his soldiers to round up the French settlers. Their homes were burned and the Acadians were loaded onto ships. Some of the ships took them to Massachusetts, Connecticut, and New York. Once they arrived in these British colonies, the Acadian children were taken from their parents and forced to become indentured servants. Others died of smallpox on a ship bound for Pennsylvania.

The EXPULSION of the ACADIANS

COLONEL JOHN WINSLOW (THE GRANDSON OF EDWARD Winslow, one of the founders of the Plymouth Colony in Massachusetts) read a proclamation to the Acadians from Governor Lawrence on September 5, 1755.

That your land and tenements [houses], cattle of all kinds and livestock are forfeited to the Crown with all other effects, saving your money and household goods, and that you yourselves to be removed from this Province . . . I am through His Majesty's goodness, directed to allow you liberty to carry your money and household goods as many as you can without [overloading] the vessels you go in.

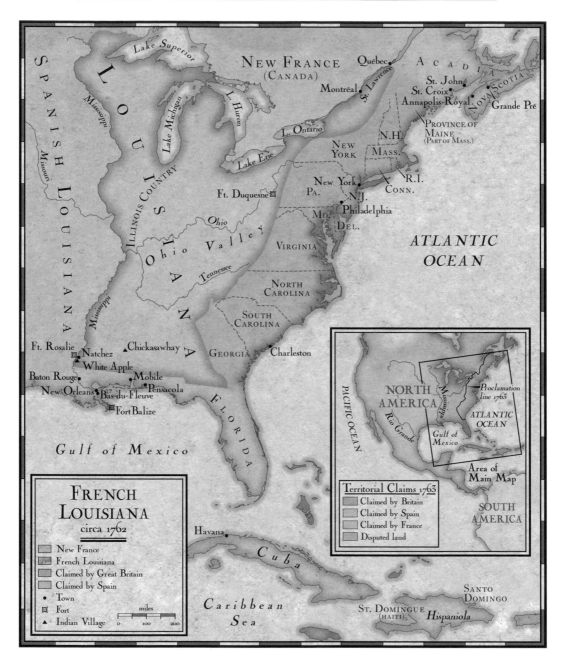

The French and Indian War cost France its empire in North America. Many French set-tlers forced from Acadia by the British found their way to Louisiana, where they settled mainly between New Orleans and Baton Rouge. France gave New Orleans and all of Louisiana west of the Mississippi River to Spain in 1762. In 1763 the Treaty of Paris gave Britain control of the rest of Louisiana, leaving St. Domingue on the island of Hispaniola France's only colony in North America (see inset map).

A few Acadian families were taken to the West Indies, islands in the Caribbean Sea, and eventually made their way to Louisiana. Others escaped to the west from Acadia and traveled down the Mississippi River to New Orleans. The first Acadian families began arriving in Louisiana during the 1760s. In Louisiana, they were called Cajuns. The Cajuns settled along the Mississippi River between New Orleans and Baton Rouge in an area that became known as the Acadian Coast. The Cajun community eventually became centered around what is present-day Lafayette.

Cajuns—name for Acadians who settled in Louisiana after being forced out of Canada

The Cajuns struggled to deal with the climate in Louisiana, which was much warmer and more humid than where they had lived in New France. They quickly discovered that crops such as wheat and corn, which they had grown in the north, did not flourish in Louisiana. The Cajuns also had to battle an epidemic of smallpox that took many lives. Nevertheless, the Cajuns eventually established successful settlements in Louisiana. They began raising cattle again and growing rice, which thrived in the Louisiana climate.

FRANCE LOSES ITS EMPIRE

The fate of the Acadians was eventually shared by all of New France. Little by little, British armies captured the French outposts. In 1759, Québec fell to the British, and a year later, Montréal was captured. In 1763, France and Britain signed the Treaty of Paris, under which France gave up the area of New France in what is now eastern Canada and all of Louisiana east of the Mississippi River. By the time the Treaty of Paris was signed, the French had already given up New Orleans. In 1762, France had signed a secret agreement with its ally Spain. Under this agreement, Spain took control of New Orleans and all of Louisiana west of the Mississippi River. The French wished to show their gratitude to Spain for its help in fighting the war. Although Spain felt that the unprofitable Louisiana colony was of little value, they accepted this gift to insure the British did not seize the region and become a threat to their holdings in Mexico.

LOUISIANA CHANGES HANDS

The French settlers in Louisiana were unhappy about the decision to give the colony to Spain. A group of leading colonists tried to prevent the colony from changing hands. They were French and wanted to be ruled from Paris. In 1765, they sent a representative to seek the help of Bienville. He was now an old man living in Paris and could do nothing to save Louisiana. About the same time, Spain appointed Don Antonio de Ulloa as the first governor of Spanish Louisiana.

Before Governor Ulloa left for Louisiana, he sent a letter to the people of New Orleans. Ulloa addressed the Superior Council, which was made up of Frenchmen who would be his advisers when he arrived in Louisiana. The new governor wrote, "*I take this occasion to inform you and to notify you that I shall soon have the honor to be among you. . . . I flatter myself beforehand that it will give me many opportunities of rendering to you all the services that you and the inhabitants of the city can wish for.*"

As Ulloa waited for a ship to take him to Louisiana, conditions in the colony following the war were growing worse. Captain Charles Aubry, the acting French governor, wrote Ulloa, "*It has been two years since we have received any supplies, our magazines [storehouses for gunpowder] are empty. I cannot give any more to the [Indians] who come from everywhere to New Orleans to find out when you will be here. . . . I await [your arrival] with the greatest impatience.*"

THE NEW GOVERNOR

Governor Ulloa finally reached New Orleans on March 5, 1766. He brought only 90 soldiers with him. Ulloa wanted Aubry and his soldiers—about 300 troops—to join the Spanish, but they refused. Aubry and his soldiers were opposed to Spanish rule and did not want to lay down their lives for an empire they did not consider themselves part of. Although Ulloa asked for more soldiers from Spain, none were sent. To gain the support of the French people, he was forced to jointly govern New Orleans with Aubry and his soldiers. On January 20, 1767, both men signed a written agreement to work together.

Ulloa was very concerned about the British. From the posts they had taken over in Pensacola and St. Marks in West Florida as a result of the 1763 Treaty of Paris, they were a threat to the Spanish in New Orleans. British ships from western Florida could easily sail along the Gulf Coast and then up the Mississippi River. Ulloa built a new fort at the mouth of the Mississippi, near Balize, called Real Catolica. Aubry complimented the Spanish governor on the new fort, writing that *"you could not have placed it in a better spot."* Ulloa also planned to build forts around New Orleans.

Soon after arriving in Louisiana, Ulloa met with chiefs of the Chickasaw, Choctaw, and other Native American peoples. He gave them presents and assured them that Spain would continue the alliances created by the French. Ulloa also wanted the fur trade, which was still controlled by French merchants, to continue. Ulloa, however, established some new rules. Each trader now had to be licensed by the Spanish government. Ulloa also prohibited trading brandy with the Indians. Finally, he ordered that no tribes should receive guns or gunpowder unless they had been given them in the past.

Ulloa also required all ships entering New Orleans to have licenses. This was an effort by the governor to stop smuggling. The governor wanted New Orleans to trade primarily with Spain and its other colonies. However, the merchants of New Orleans had been smuggling goods from British colonies into Louisiana to sell at high prices. They were opposed to Ulloa's new laws.

Ships sailing up the Mississippi River were greeted by the sight of a Spanish fort called Real Catolica, built at the mouth of the river by Governor Ulloa to protect Spain's interests in New Orleans and the Louisiana colony.

For the politically powerful merchants, the economic situation in Louisiana gradually grew worse. Meanwhile, the Spanish government failed to send Ulloa enough money to pay the soldiers properly or buy presents for the Native

Americans. This led to problems with his Indian allies. At the end of 1767, he wrote, *"I want to reiterate . . . the poverty of this country due to the lack of funds, having used the last and being without even the necessary means for daily needs; nobody can be paid, the troops, the body of officers, clerks, and the providers [merchants]."*

A REVOLT BEGINS

Many colonists were upset by the poor economy in Louisiana, and the economic problems soon led to revolt. The rebellion against Governor Ulloa was led by Nicolas Foucault, the French commissary-general, the official in charge of supplies. He was joined by the chief legal officer in Louisiana, French attorney-general, Nicolas Chauvin de La Freniere. Foucault was a smuggler who was losing money because of Ulloa's new laws. As a popular member of the Superior Council, which was still mostly made up of Frenchmen and which ran the colony along with the Spanish governor, La Freniere had the power to convince other councilors to go along with his ideas.

Foucault and La Freniere started planning to overthrow Ulloa during the summer of 1768. They received strong support from many merchants. German farmers in Louisiana who had not been paid for food they had supplied to the government also joined the revolt. La Freniere urged the Supreme Council to send Ulloa away. *"Where is the liberty of our planters, our merchants and our other inhabitants?"*

he said. Late in October, the Supreme Council voted to force Ulloa from the colony. Although Aubry protested the council's decision, he did nothing to change it. On November 1, Ulloa sailed from New Orleans to the Spanish colony of Cuba. He never returned to Louisiana.

THE REACTION OF THE SPANISH

After Ulloa had gone, the leaders of the revolt wrote a long letter to the French government of Louis XV in Paris. The ringleaders urged France to take back control of Louisiana. They criticized the Spanish economic policies and explained that Louisiana could be a profitable colony for France. A group of colonists sailed to Paris to meet with the French government, but France had no interest in Louisiana.

Economic conditions did not improve in Louisiana. A few wealthy merchants prospered by smuggling and selling goods outside the colony, and large plantation owners were able to turn a profit from the export of rice, indigo, and tobacco, but the majority of colonists were still struggling along the frontiers of Louisiana. Many people who had supported the revolt against Ulloa now began to change their minds. Governor Aubry said, *"The people are [sorry]. The part [power] of the rebels grows smaller every day."* Aubry predicted that a small force of about 300 men could easily enable Spain to take back control of Louisiana.

A portrait of General Alexander O'Reilly, the Irish soldier who commanded the Spanish Army that retook New Orleans from the French

The Spanish were already planning to retake the colony. They felt that Louisiana acted as a buffer, protecting the Spanish colonies in California and Mexico against Britain's colonies in Florida and along the eastern banks of the Mississippi River. In 1769, Spain raised an army under the command of General Alexander O'Reilly.

O'Reilly arrived at the mouth of the Mississippi River in July with more than 2,000 soldiers. Governor Aubry immediately sent word that he was ready to let the Spanish take back control of Louisiana. Several French colonists went to meet with O'Reilly. Among them was La Freniere. He told O'Reilly that the French in Louisiana wanted to remain a colony of Spain. La Freniere added that only the policies of Governor Ulloa had caused the settlers to revolt. O'Reilly listened to the settlers. *"Gentlemen, it is not possible for me to judge things without first finding out about the prior circumstances,"* he said. *"I shall devote all my attention to becoming informed about everything thoroughly."*

Once O'Reilly arrived in New Orleans, he took control of the colony. Aubry gave him the names of the leaders of the revolt. On August 21, General O'Reilly had these men thrown into prison. The men were tried and found guilty. Some, including La Freniere, were sentenced to death. On October 25, 1769, they were taken before a firing squad. *"They were well dressed,"* said an observer, *"and perfectly calm and self-possessed . . . looking around them kindly and returning salutes addressed to them."* La Freniere yelled out before his death, *"I am French! The cry of liberty has been heard!"* Spain, however, had easily succeeded in regaining control of Louisiana. ※

CHAPTER EIGHT

Life in Spanish Louisiana

SPAIN GOVERNS LOUISIANA UNTIL *the end of the 18th century, when it is turned back to France, before being sold to the United States in 1803.*

fter General O'Reilly took back control of Louisiana, he strengthened the Spanish government there. The population and the economy of Louisiana grew steadily over the next two decades. As governor of Louisiana, O'Reilly made it clear to the people of New Orleans that they were now subjects of Spain. O'Reilly removed the French Superior Council, which had

OPPOSITE: White Hall Plantation in Louisiana, built by a Spanish settler around 1790, can still be visited today.

helped overthrow Ulloa. He replaced it with a cabildo. Its members were wealthy citizens of New Orleans who were loyal to Spain, and consisted of French and Spanish men. Many members of the cabildo were appointed for

cabildo—a government advisory council in the Spanish colonies

life. The cabildo handled a variety of duties, such as maintaining levees to prevent floods, enforcing slave codes, and overseeing the city jail.

The French Market in New Orleans did a brisk Sunday business. Settlers could purchase meat, fruits and vegetables, and spices to cook with.

NEW ORLEANS—
A THRIVING CITY

Under the Spanish, New Orleans continued as the capital and economic center of Louisiana. The city grew from a population of barely 400 at the end of French and Indian War to 6,000 by the 1790s and became a more successful trading center. Merchants grew even wealthier by exporting agricultural products to Europe and importing European goods. Carpenters, blacksmiths, and other artisans found work in New Orleans, building homes for the wealthy and setting up shops to handle the growing commerce. The city government expanded, employing more officials. As a result of these changes, more money was available to support a richer cultural life.

By 1788, the city had one private school for girls and eight schools that taught a total of more than 400 boys. In addition, a special school was opened to educate young men for the Spanish Army. Well-to-do men joined the city militia, in part because they enjoyed wearing military uniforms. Historian Christina Vella writes that *"men loved splendid shirts and jackets . . . They [owned] dozens of velvet and silk suits in black, crimson, and scarlet. . . . Men wore wigs and hair powder until the first five years of the nineteenth century."*

Nevertheless, New Orleans was not as well developed as cities like New York or Philadelphia, Pennsylvania, in the newly independent United States. Water from the

Mississippi River often flowed over the levees into the city, so the streets were regularly flooded. Alligators and poisonous snakes sometimes swam in the streets through smelly garbage that collected there. Bodies washed out of local cemeteries and could be seen floating in the water.

Wooden sidewalks built above the water allowed residents to get to shops and markets as well as to more than 90 taverns where people drank and gambled. There were cafés that served tea and coffee. In 1792, New Orleans opened a theater where plays and opera were performed. Residents often spent Sunday afternoons attending a game called toli, introduced by the Choctaw Indians. Teams of men, each carrying two short sticks, tried to knock a ball between a set of goalposts. Sometimes, Choctaw teams competed against teams of white settlers.

toli—a Choctaw game played in New Orleans

Beginning in the 1790s, streetlamps lit with candles were put up along the sidewalks in New Orleans to light the way. Swarms of mosquitoes and other insects constantly circled the lights. These mosquitoes carried diseases such as malaria and yellow fever. Malaria epidemics regularly broke out, killing many people in New Orleans.

The city was also struck by hurricanes and fires. One fire broke out on March 21, 1788. Since the buildings in New Orleans were made mostly of cypress wood, the fire spread rapidly with the help of a strong wind. More than 800 buildings—most of the city—were destroyed.

Although the buildings were replaced, another fire devastated part of New Orleans in 1794.

Don Andres Almonester

Much of the rebuilding in New Orleans after the fires of 1788 and 1794 was financed by Don Andres Almonester. Born near Seville, Spain, in 1728, Almonester later moved to Madrid, Spain's capital. There he began to build a fortune, first by investing money in real estate and later by building houses.

In 1769, Almonester left Spain for New Orleans, though it is unknown why he went to North America. Once again, he began buying property and constructing rental apartments. By the early 1780s, Almonester owned valuable real estate in the center of New Orleans. As his building projects increased, Almonester employed more than 100 slaves to work on them. He became the richest man in New Orleans.

Due to his great wealth, Almonester was selected as a member of the cabildo. After the fire of 1788, Almonester financed the rebuilding of the headquarters of the cabildo, a public school, and a hospital. He also directed the rebuilding of New Orleans after the 1794 fire. He died in 1798.

A FRENCH VISITOR

AT THE BEGINNING OF THE 19TH century, C.C. Robin visited New Orleans from France. In his book *Voyage to Louisiana*, Robin wrote that *"the principal occupation [of New Orleans] is that of commerce."* With the money made in trade, merchants and well-to-do planters put on lavish balls at their houses. New Orleans women, dressed in beautiful ball gowns, often walked through the muddy streets in their bare feet on their way to house parties. One of the things that most amazed Robin was the diet of the New Orleans people. *"There is no country on earth where so much meat is consumed in proportion to the number of inhabitants. . . . At every table they serve small pieces of bread and huge pieces of meat. The amount which the children of the people consume would startle a European."*

IMPACT OF THE REVOLUTIONARY WAR ON LOUISIANA

In 1770, O'Reilly left Louisiana and turned over the colony to a new governor, Don Louis de Unzaga. While O'Reilly had forbidden smuggling, the new governor permitted it to resume. French traders began selling indigo, furs, and timber to British posts at Natchez and in western Florida. As a result, the economy of the colony improved even more.

In 1775, war broke out between Britain and its American colonies, which wanted independence from the empire. Three years later, France joined the war as an ally of the Americans. While Britain was fighting both France and the colonists, Spain declared war on Britain in 1779. From Louisiana, the Spanish launched an expedition aimed at regaining some of the outposts they had lost to the British in the French and Indian War.

Led by a new governor, Bernardo de Galvez, the Spanish Army retook Natchez. Galvez also wanted to retake western Florida. In February, the governor sailed from Balize and captured Mobile in March 1780. He then assembled a large force and marched against Pensacola. This town fell to the Spanish a year later. In 1783, Britain signed a peace treaty recognizing the independence of their former thirteen colonies as the United States of America. The British signed another treaty giving western Florida back to Spain and allowing the Spanish to hold onto Natchez and Mobile.

While Louisiana had been founded to carry on the fur trade, by the time the American war for independence ended, its commerce had become largely dependent on agriculture. Louisiana planters grew tobacco, rice, and indigo for shipment overseas. During the 1790s, a Louisiana planter named Étienne de Boré began experimenting with sugar. He developed a method to produce granulated sugar from the juice of sugarcane grown on his plantation. By the beginning of the 19th century, New Orleans planters were making 4.5 million pounds (2 million kg) of sugar each year. Cotton production was also increasing. In the 1790s, American inventor Eli Whitney developed the cotton gin. With this device, seeds could be removed rapidly from balls of cotton. As a result, cotton plantations began to grow around Louisiana. In order to support the expansion of

Upper South—
Virginia, North
Carolina, Maryland,
Kentucky, and
Tennessee

cotton and sugar production, Louisiana planters had to find more slaves. The planters found them not only in Africa, but also from wealthy American landowners in the Upper South.

Africans in New Orleans

The huge job of rebuilding New Orleans after the fires required the work of many African slaves. Some earned extra money working for the city as carpenters and brick-layers. A few even earned enough money to buy their freedom. From 1791 until the beginning of the 19th century, the number of free African Americans in New Orleans increased from about 850 to more than 1,800.

Nevertheless, the majority of blacks remained enslaved. During the period of Spanish control, the number of slaves in Louisiana rose from about 5,000 in 1763 to 24,000 in 1800. Slave ships brought an increasing number of Africans to New Orleans to work on the plantations or as household slaves. Under the Spanish, the Code Noir was changed to allow slave families to be broken up and children to be sold to other masters. In addition, slaves were regularly whipped by their masters.

One slave named Antoine described how an overseer *"fell upon us [Antoine and his friends] with great blows of a branch which he cut from a tree with an ax. We all decided to go maroon."* A large maroon community

Maroon—a
fugitive Black slave

of former slaves arose along the Mississippi River, south of New Orleans. Known as Bas-du-Fleuve, the community had approximately 2,500 residents by about 1780. The inhabitants grew vegetables to feed themselves. The maroons also cut cypress logs. They sold these to sawmill owners who milled the logs into boards for building houses.

As cotton production increased in the early 1800s, more slaves were needed to work the huge plantations that grew this profitable crop. Two overseers keep watchful eye on slaves picking cotton from the fields on a plantation in Louisiana.

Many of the maroons carried weapons. Louisiana planters worried that the former slaves might revolt and attack the white settlers. Among the leaders of the maroons was Juan Malo, known as Saint Malo. During the 1780s, the

Spanish tried to capture Saint Malo, but they were unsuccessful. Eventually, the Spanish put up a large reward for
Saint Malo's capture. In 1784, his hideout was located with
the help of a group of free blacks employed by the colonial
government. Saint Malo was captured, tried, and executed.

A Colony No Longer

In 1800, Spain handed the colony of Louisiana back to
France. Emperor Napoleon I persuaded Spain to give
Louisiana to France in return for some territory in Europe.
Napoleon wanted to rebuild France's empire in North
America. The plan was to retake control of its colony of St.
Domingue (now Haiti), which had been lost in a slave
uprising. From there he would launch an attack on
Louisiana. When President Thomas Jefferson realized what
Napoleon was up to, he was afraid that the French emperor
would try to close the port of New Orleans and interfere
with trade on the Mississippi.

The French Army sent to St. Domingue was quickly
defeated by the local rebels. Napoleon, occupied with a
major war in Europe, could not spare his attention to main-
tain an empire in America. President Jefferson told his
ambassador to France, Robert Livingston, to try to persuade the French emperor to sell New Orleans to the United
States. Congress set aside as much as $2 million to purchase
the city.

Napoleon wanted to sell all of Louisiana to the United States for a larger price. The United States agreed to purchase the territory from France for $15 million. The Louisiana Purchase (see map below) covered almost 800,000 acres (324,000 ha), including the present-day states of Oklahoma, Arkansas, Missouri, Iowa, Kansas, Nebraska and South Dakota, as well as parts of Minnesota, North Dakota, Montana, Wyoming, Colorado, New Mexico, Texas, and, of course, Louisiana. Even though Louisiana became a U.S. territory in 1803, its mixture of Old World cultures endured. Even today, Louisiana remains a distinctive product of its colorful past. ❈

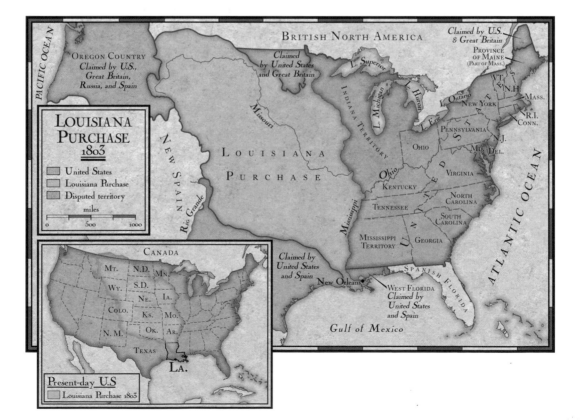

TIME LINE

1682 René-Robert Cavelier, Sieur de La Salle, claims Louisiana for France.

1699 Pierre Le Moyne, Sieur d' Iberville, establishes the first French settlement in Louisiana.

1702 The French build a settlement at Mobile.

1706 Iberville dies in Havana, Cuba. Jean-Baptiste Le Moyne, Sieur de Bienville becomes governor of Louisiana.

1712 Antoine Crozat takes control of Louisiana.

1714 Bienville establishes Fort Toulouse in what is now Alabama.

1716 Bienville establishes Fort Rosalie in Natchez, in what is now Mississippi.

1717 The Mississippi Company takes over Louisiana.

1718 Bienville builds New Orleans.

1719 African slaves begin arriving in Louisiana.

1722 New Orleans becomes the capital of Louisiana.

1729 The Natchez Indians revolt.

1731 The Mississippi Company gives up Louisiana.

1732 Bienville becomes governor of Louisiana for the second time.

1743 Pierre de Rigaud de Vaudreuil becomes governor of Louisiana.

1754 The French and Indian War begins. It ends nine years later.

1755 The Acadians are driven out of New France. Some go to Louisiana.

1762 A secret treaty transfers Louisiana from French to Spanish rule.

1768 French settlers oust the Spanish governor, Don Antonio de Ulloa.

1769 Spain reasserts control of Louisiana.

1779–1781 Spain retakes Natchez, Mobile, and Pensacola from Great Britain.

1788 A great fire destroys much of New Orleans.

1794 Another fire devastates New Orleans.

1800 Spain gives Louisiana to France in exchange for territory in Europe.

1803 The French emperor, Napoleon I, sells Louisiana to the United States. Louisiana becomes a U.S. territory.

RESOURCES

BOOKS

Brasseaux, Carl A. *The Founding of New Acadia: The Beginnings of Acadian Life in Louisiana, 1765–1803.* Baton Rouge: Louisiana State University Press, 1997.

*Din, Gilbert, and John Harkins. *The New Orleans Cabildo.* Baton Rouge: Louisiana State University Press, 1996.

Eckberg, Carl. *French Roots in the Illinois Country.* Urbana: University of Illinois Press, 2000.

Hale, Duane, and Arrell Gibson. *The Chickasaw.* Philadelphia: Chelsea House, 1991.

Hall, Gwendolyn Midlo. *Africans in Colonial Louisiana.* Baton Rouge: Louisiana State University Press, 1992.

McKee, Jesse. *The Choctaw.* Philadelphia: Chelsea House, 1989.

*Usner, Daniel. *Indians, Settlers, and Slaves in a Frontier Exchange Economy: The Lower Mississippi Valley Before 1783.* Chapel Hill, N.C.: University of North Carolina Press, 1992.

Vella, Christina. *Intimate Enemies: The Two Worlds of the Baroness De Pontalba.* Baton Rouge: Louisiana State University Press, 1997.

Wall, Bennet H. Louisiana: *A History Wheeling, Illinois:* Harlan Davidson, 1990.

*college-level sources

WEB SITES

Dictionary of Canadian Biography Online
http://www.biographi.ca/
This online dictionary is an excellent source for biographical material on Pierre de Rigaud de Vaudreuil de Cavagnal.

Enchanted Learning—René-Robert Cavelier, Sieur de La Salle: North American Explorer
http://www.enchantedlearning.com/explorers/page/l/lasalle.shtml
This Web site provides a valuable introduction to the life of La Salle.

The Library of Congress Presents America's Story from America's Library
http://www.americaslibrary.gov/cgi-bin/page.cgi
The Library of Congress's Web page for kids contains fascinating information on Louisiana and the American colonies.

New Advent Catholic Encyclopedia—Antoine de Lamothe, Sieur de Cadillac
www.newadvent.org/cathen/03131a.htm
This Web page contains an in-depth biography of Cadillac.

New Orleans Gateway—Jean Baptiste Le Moyne, Sieur de Bienville
www.gatewayno.com/history/Bienville.html
There is an excellent introduction to the life of Bienville, a founder of Louisiana, on this Web page.

QUOTE SOURCES

CHAPTER ONE

p. 16 "stubborn…tempered." Johnson, Donald. *LaSalle*. New York: Cooper Square Press, 2002, p.28; p.19 "Louis…1682." Johnson, p. 111.

CHAPTER TWO

p. 29 "All the…baggage." http://www.datasync.com/~david g59/biloxil.html. Pierre LeMoyne Sieur d'Iberville and the Establishment of Biloxi; "When drawing…strong current." http://www.datasync.com/~david g59/biloxil.html. Pierre LeMoyne Sieur d'Iberville and the Establishment of Biloxi; p. 33 "more than…war parties." Unser, Daniel H. *Indians, Settlers, and Slaves in a Frontier Exchange Economy: The Lower Mississippi Valley Before 1783*. Chapel Hill, North Carolina: University of North Carolina Press, 1990, p. 19.

CHAPTER THREE

p. 38 "a wretched…vegetables." Johnson, Donald. *LaSalle*. New York: Cooper Square Press, 2002, p. 164; "According…religion." Johnson, p. 164; p. 46 "At that…lodged." Roberts, W. Adolphe. *Lake Ponchartrain*. New York: Bobbs Merrill, 1946, pp. 37–38; "lodged me…wild country." Roberts, pp. 37–38; p. 48 "Although great…produced death." Unser, Daniel H. *Indians, Settlers, and Slaves in a Frontier Exchange Economy: The Lower Mississippi Valley Before 1783*. Chapel Hill, North Carolina: University of North Carolina Press, 1990, p.36; p. 51 "The city…sight as Paris." Roberts, p. 82.

CHAPTER FOUR

p. 54 "In a word…gold or silver." Hall, Gwendolyn Midlo. *Africans in Colonial Louisiana*. Baton Rouge: Louisiana State University Press, 1992, p. 37; p. 56 "Moluron…I'll escape." Hall, p. 142; p. 59 "all slaves…Catholic religion." http://www.top-tags.com/aama/docs/lublkcodes.htm. The Black Code of Louisiana, March 1724; "slaves belonging…whip." http://www.toptags.com/aama/docs/lublkcodes.htm. The Black Code of Louisiana, March 1724.

CHAPTER FIVE

p. 67 "for too long…to be shed." Unser, Daniel H. *Indians, Settlers, and Slaves in a Frontier Exchange Economy: The Lower Mississippi Valley Before 1783*. Chapel Hill, North Carolina: University of North Carolina Press, 1990, p.88; p. 68 "All the…as he likes." Unser, p. 89; "was given…present." Unser, p. 89; "the principal…Choctaw villages." Unser, p. 89; "those who…do not fear." Unser, pp. 88–89; p. 69 "Le Normant…arrangements." http://www.biographi.ca/EN/ShowBioPrintable.asp?BIOID=36264. Dictionary of Canadian Biography, "Rigaud de Vaudreuil."

CHAPTER SIX

p. 76 "No trips…oar in hand." Ekbert, Carl J. *French Roots in the Illinois Country*. Urbana, Illinois: University of Illinois Press, 2000, p. 281.

CHAPTER SEVEN

p. 81 "That your land…you go in." http:john.doucette.com/Acadian/Acadian proclamation.html; p. 85 "I take…can wish for." Moore, John Preston. *Revolt in Louisiana: The Spanish Occupation, 1766–1770*. Baton Rouge: Louisiana State University Press, 1976, p. 12; "It has been…greatest impatience." Moore, p. 13; p. 86 "You…spot." Moore, p. 71; p. 88 "I want to…the providers [merchants]." Moore, p. 128; p. 88; "Where is…other inhabitants?" Roberts, W. Adolphe. *Lake Ponchartrain*. New York: Bobbs Merrill, 1946, p. 83; p. 89 "The people…every day." Moore, p. 183; p. 90 "Gentlemen…everything thoroughly." Roberts, pp. 196–197; p. 91 "They were…addressed to them." Roberts, p. 89; "I am…been heard!" Roberts, p. 89.

CHAPTER EIGHT

p. 95 "men loved…nineteenth century." Vella, Christina. *Intimate Enemies*. Baton Rouge: Louisiana State University Press, 1997, p. 34; p.98 "the principal…of commerce." Phelps, Albert. *Louisiana*. Boston: Houghton Mifflin, 1905, p. 211; "There is no…startle a European." Phelps, p. 211; p. 100 "fell upon…to go maroon." Hall, Gwendolyn Midlo. *Africans in Colonial Louisiana*. Baton Rouge: Louisiana State University Press, 1992, p. 204.

INDEX

ABOUT THE AUTHOR
AND CONSULTANT

RICHARD WORTH has written several biographies and histories for middle graders, including *Thomas Nast, Henry VIII, Stanley and Livingston, Ponce de Leon, Pizarro, Westward Expansion and Manifest Destiny, Women in Combat,* and *The Spanish Inquisition.* He lives in Fairfield, Connecticut.

KEVIN D. ROBERTS is an assistant professor of history at New Mexico State University. He earned his Ph.D. in colonial American/African-American history at the University of Texas at Austin, where his thesis examined African-American culture and the influence of slavery on the transition of Louisiana from a French to a Spanish colony, and finally to a territory under American governance. He has published numerous articles and chapters on various aspects of race and history in the South. His ancestors hail from one of the original Creole families of Louisiana.

ILLUSTRATION CREDITS

NORTH AMERICA Divided into its III PRINCIPALL PARTS 1st ENGLISH Part Viz ENGLISH EMPIRE containin
N Foundland N Scotland N England N York N Jarsey Pensylvania Maryland Virginia Carolina Carolania or Florida California, Sommer Is Bahama Is Jamaica &c. Carib Is II SPANISH Viz N Sp

1685